ROCKETS and SATELLITES

Troll Associates

ROCKETS and SATELLITES

by Francene Sabin

Illustrated by R. Maccabe

Troll Associates

Library of Congress Cataloging in Publication Data
Sabin, Francene.
　　Rockets and satellites.

　　Summary: Discusses rocketry technology as it relates to the launching of satellites and the limitless usefulness of artificial satellites.
　　1. Rocketry—Juvenile literature.　2. Artificial satellites—Juvenile literature.　[1. Rocketry.　2. Artificial satellites]　I. Maccabe, Richard, ill.　II. Title.
TL782.5.S225　　1985　　　629.47′5　　　84-2738
ISBN 0-8167-0288-8 (lib. bdg.)
ISBN 0-8167-0289-6 (pbk.)

Copyright © 1985 by Troll Associates, Mahwah, New Jersey
All rights reserved. No part of this book may be used
or reproduced in any manner whatsoever without written
permission from the publisher.
Printed in the United States of America
10　9　8　7　6　5　4　3　2　1

Before 1957, there was only one satellite circling the Earth. It was our natural satellite, the moon. But today, there are many other satellites speeding around this planet. Unlike the moon, they are artificial satellites, placed in orbit by people.

Some transmit information that is used for weather forecasting. Some are used to bounce radio, television, and telephone signals back to Earth. Some gather information about space, solar radiation, or the geography of our planet. Artificial satellites have quickly become important tools of modern technology and science.

But it took rocketry, another creation of modern technology, to put these satellites into orbit. Rockets are the engines that propel satellites into Earth orbit and lift spacecraft to the moon and beyond. The rockets that do these tasks are very large, complicated, and costly. But the way they work is basically the same as any Fourth of July rocket used for fireworks.

Essentially, a rocket is a tube filled with fuel. The tube has one open end and one closed end. When the fuel is burned, it turns into gas, which rushes out the open end of the tube. This pushes the tube in the opposite direction.

Long before anyone understood why a rocket works, people were making and launching them. Scientists believe the first rockets were invented almost 1,000 years ago in China.

Rocketry reached Europe 200 to 300 years after its invention in China. Rockets were used as weapons in many European wars. But not until the twentieth century did scientists develop the technology to send rockets great distances.

The scientific principles on which all rockets work are known as the *three laws of motion.* Together with the *law of universal gravitation,* they explain how all rockets and satellites operate. The laws of motion and gravity were contributed by Sir Isaac Newton, a seventeenth-century English scientist.

Newton's first law of motion states that a body at rest will remain at rest until some force moves it. The law goes on to state that a body moving in a straight line will continue moving in a straight line unless some force makes it change direction. This first law of motion is also called the principle of inertia.

Newton's second law of motion states that a moving body changes its motion in relation to the force causing the change. In other words, a small push causes a small change of direction, and a large push causes a greater change of direction. Newton's second law also states that the body moves in the direction dictated by the force.

Newton's third law of motion, which is particularly important to the understanding of rocketry, might be called the law of

action and reaction. It states that for every action, there is an equal and opposite reaction.

An example of this law is what happens when a person dives into a lake from a floating rowboat. As the person dives forward, the rowboat is pushed backward. The action—diving forward—produces an equal and opposite reaction—the backward movement of the rowboat.

Newton's law of universal gravitation was based on the theories of a German scientist named Johannes Kepler. Kepler's laws of planetary motion described the way planets and moons orbit in space. Newton proved mathematically that Kepler's laws were correct. Newton then explained that Kepler's laws operated because of gravity.

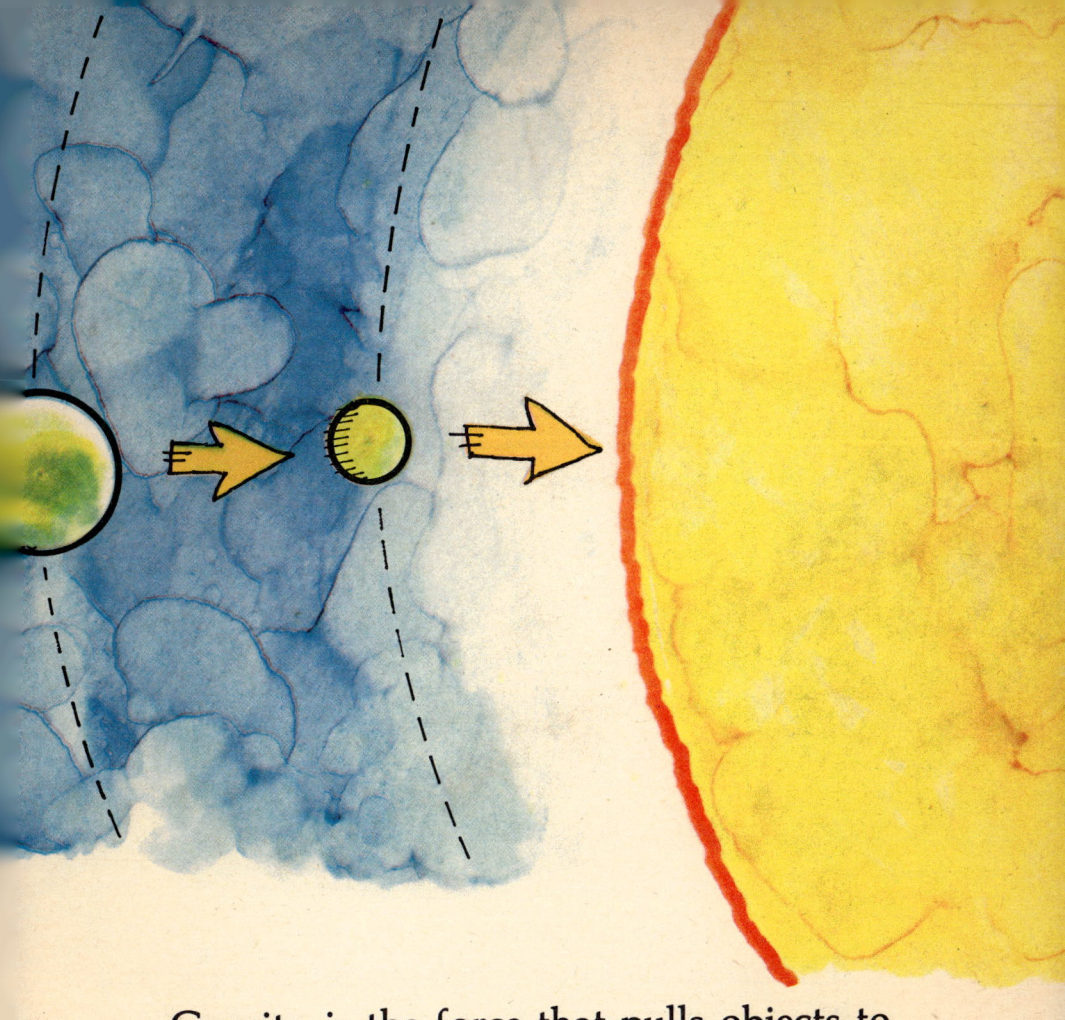

Gravity is the force that pulls objects to Earth and gives weight to objects. Gravity is also exerted by every other planet, moon, and star in the universe. For example, the gravity of the sun keeps the planets from flying off into space. And the gravitational attraction of the Earth keeps our moon in orbit.

The artificial satellites that circle the Earth today are held in orbit by two natural forces. One force is inertia, which makes a moving satellite continue to move in the same direction it is moving, unless some force causes it to change direction. The other force is the force of the Earth's gravity, which pulls the satellite toward Earth and keeps it from flying off into space.

In order to place an artificial satellite in orbit, the power of a rocket is required. The function of the rocket is explained by Newton's third law of motion. That is, the law of action and reaction. The expanding gas, rushing out the open end of the rocket, is the action. The rocket shooting forward is the reaction. This forward motion is called a rocket's thrust.

The thrust of a rocket is what carries a satellite beyond the Earth's atmosphere. But since the force of gravity is acting against the rocket, the thrust must be strong enough to overcome the force of gravity.

Rocket technology is a development of the twentieth century. In 1903, a Russian named Konstantin Tsiolkovsky published a scientific paper that described how rockets might reach beyond Earth's atmosphere.

But not until 1926 was the first practical rocket built. It was the invention of an American physicist, Dr. Robert Goddard. Goddard's rocket, fueled by a mixture of gasoline and liquid oxygen, flew only a brief time and only a short distance, but it marked the birth of the Rocket Age.

Rocket technology improved over the next decades. In Germany, a team of scientists, under the direction of Wernher von Braun, developed a series of rockets able to fly long distances with considerable accuracy. After World War II, von Braun and a number of his co-workers came to the United States to continue their work with rockets.

There are a number of problems to deal with in launching a satellite by rocket. The first of these is weight. This weight is made up of the rocket, its fuel, and the satellite.

Heavy rockets need more thrust to place them in orbit.

The weight of the satellite, or of any rocket-powered craft, is called the payload. Obviously, the larger and heavier the payload, the larger and heavier its rockets must be. And the heavier these are, the more fuel is needed to thrust the payload into space. Another factor is that this great mass has a great inertia, or resistance, to the thrust. This means there must be a powerful blast to lift a rocket-powered craft off the ground.

The solutions to these problems have involved the development of lightweight metals and plastics for the rocket's skin, and lighter fuels for burning. Hydrogen, the lightest of all gases, produces a powerful thrust. But as a gas it takes up a large amount of room. When it is compressed into a liquid form, however, it takes up less room. That is why hydrogen, frozen to the temperature of 423 degrees below zero Fahrenheit, is used as one of the elements of rocket fuel.

There are also combination fuels, so-called because they are part liquid and part solid. These combination fuels use liquid oxygen and a solid material high in hydrogen content. Liquid oxygen cannot be stored in a rocket before use. It can explode too easily, so it is added to the rocket just before launch.

In order to carry a heavy payload, satellites are generally powered by two or three rockets. These are fired in stages. The first stage is fired to lift the satellite from the ground. When the first stage has completed its job and the desired altitude has been reached, the first-stage rocket is cast off. This lightens the payload.

The second stage is fired to provide thrust. When its fuel is used up, it, too, is cast off. With each stage, the payload becomes lighter. At the same time, the gravitational pull on the payload diminishes, so less power is needed for thrust. The last stage moves the satellite fastest, carries it farthest, and finally places the satellite in orbit. It can also send a satellite or spacecraft toward another planet or to the moon.

Rockets are steered by changing the direction of the exhaust, which is the gas shooting out the open end. Anytime the exhaust flow's direction is changed, the rocket's direction is changed.

When the *Apollo* astronauts traveled to the moon, they also needed another kind of rocket, called a retrorocket, to slow the spacecraft. The Apollo spacecraft had to be slowed enough for it to enter the moon's gravitational field and go into orbit around the moon. Otherwise, the craft would have continued moving right past the moon and out into space.

Since 1957, when the Russians launched *Sputnik 1*, there has been a steady succession of satellites sent into space. Some of these have carried human crews. Others have traveled deep into our solar system without crews.

The majority of satellites, however, do not travel very far into space. They orbit the Earth and do many jobs. Some of them allow us to watch television programs being broadcast from the other side of the world. The television signals are sent up to a satellite and bounced back to other parts of the Earth.

Artificial satellites are also used for radio transmissions and for telephone and telex communications. Still other satellites orbiting the Earth provide information about weather by sending pictures and other data of changing atmospheric conditions.

Rocket and satellite technology have contributed enormously to human knowledge. And it is clear that this technology is just beginning. The future of rocketry and satellites holds the possibilities of exploration into deep space, of permanent space stations used for scientific research and observation, of medical advances possible only in conditions offered by outer space. Because of rockets and satellites, the world of the future is filled with limitless promise.